Popular Teaching Resources

Global Warming

Grades 1-3

Contents

Global Warming **1-3**
Grades

Our
Natural World

The Atmosphere

Our **Earth** is surrounded by **a layer of gases** that we call the **atmosphere**.

The sun gives off **rays of heat**. They travel through the atmosphere to reach the Earth. The rays of the sun heat the Earth. Some of the heat from the Earth then travels back into the atmosphere. However, the gases in the atmosphere stop some of the heat from escaping into space.

Together, the sun, the atmosphere, and the Earth create the "**greenhouse effect**". It is called "greenhouse effect" because it works in just the same way as a greenhouse.

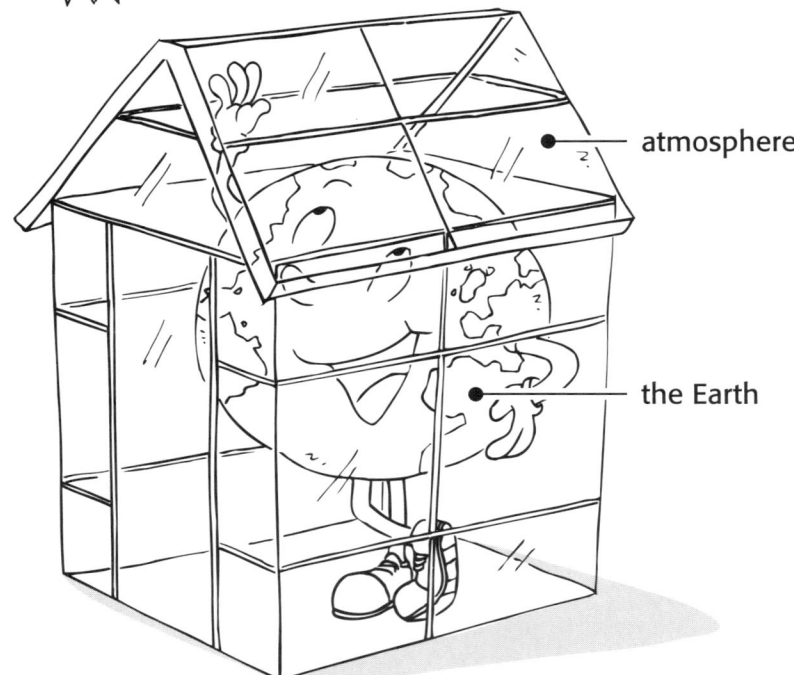

atmosphere

the Earth

Our atmosphere is like the glass panels in a greenhouse. It protects life on Earth by absorbing **ultraviolet rays** (UV rays) from the sun. Ultraviolet rays are harmful to us. The atmosphere also keeps the heat from escaping back into space. That way, it keeps the temperatures from rising too high during the day and from getting too low at night.

Because of the atmosphere, the temperature of our Earth remains constant at an average of 15°C. In contrast, the moon's average surface temperature is only -18°C because there is no atmosphere surrounding the moon.

It is because of the atmosphere that living things on Earth can survive.

The Atmosphere

Label the diagram with the given words. Then colour the thermometer to show the average temperature of the Earth.

atmosphere
sun's rays
trapped
reflected

1.

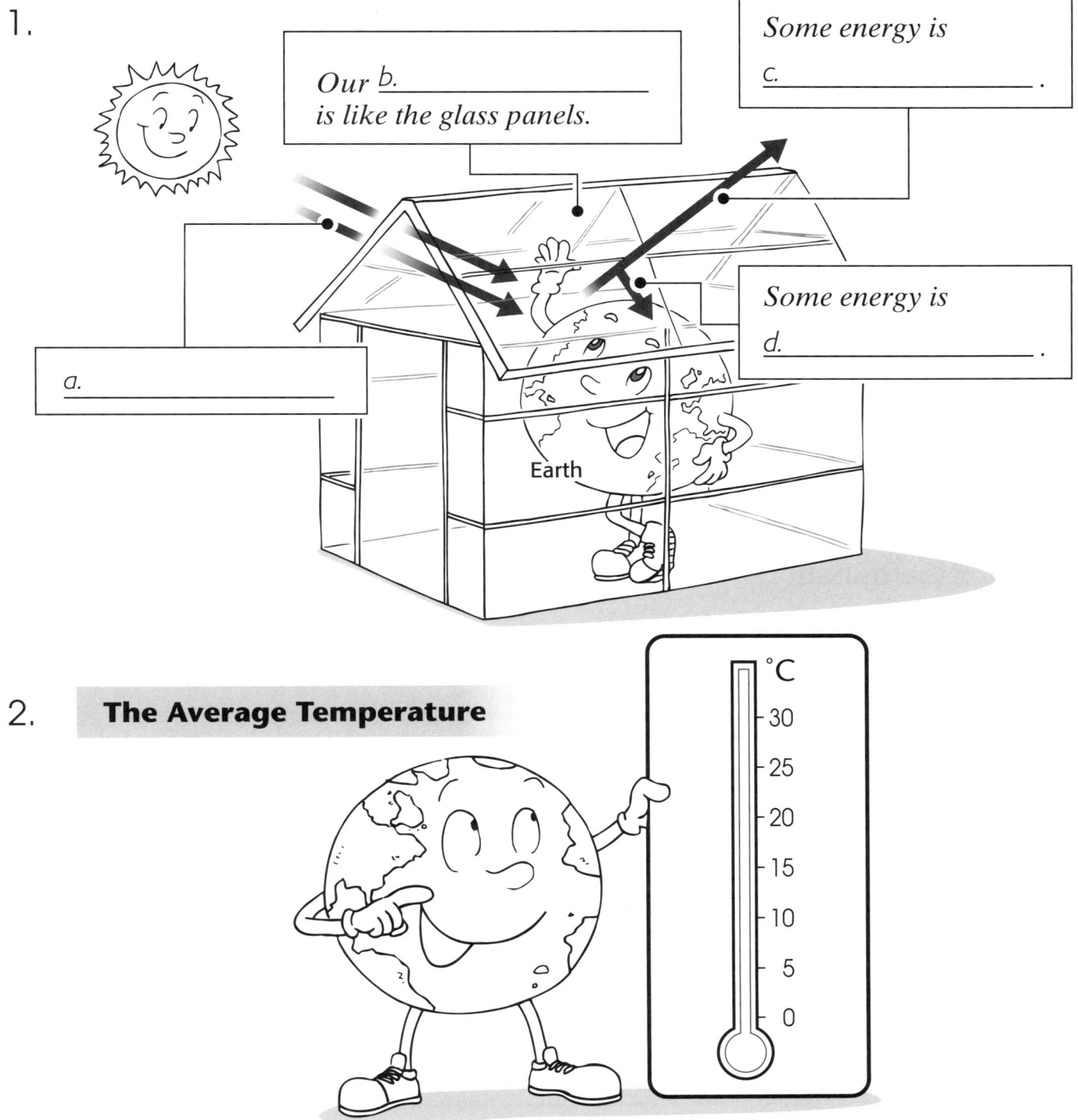

Our b. _____
is like the glass panels.

Some energy is
c. _____ .

Some energy is
d. _____ .

a. _____

Earth

2. **The Average Temperature**

°C
30
25
20
15
10
5
0

The Atmosphere

Put a check mark ✔ in the circle if the sentence is correct; otherwise, put a cross ✗.

1. The atmosphere gives off rays of heat.   ◯

2. The atmosphere covers a part of the Earth.   ◯

3. The gases in the atmosphere trap the heat that is
    trying to escape into space.   ◯

4. Carbon dioxide is one of the greenhouse gases.   ◯

5. The atmosphere helps maintain the temperature of
    the Earth.   ◯

6. The atmosphere absorbs ultraviolet rays from the sun.   ◯

Answer the questions.

7. Why is the atmosphere important to us?

    _____

    _____

8. If there were no atmosphere, what would happen to the life
    on Earth?

    _____

    _____

The Atmosphere

Colour the picture as specified. Trace the dotted lines. Then label the arrows with the correct sentences. Write the letters.

- the sun – yellow
- the Earth – blue
- the atmosphere – green

A   Solar energy is absorbed by the Earth's surface.

B   Some of the sun's rays are reflected by the Earth and the atmosphere.

C   Some of the sun's rays are absorbed and re-emitted in all directions by greenhouse gases.

The Greenhouse Effect

Water Cycle

All the water that is on Earth is the same as it always was and always will be. It keeps going around and around in what we call the "**Water Cycle**".

Water is a substance that exists in solid, liquid, and gas forms. Here is how the water cycle works:

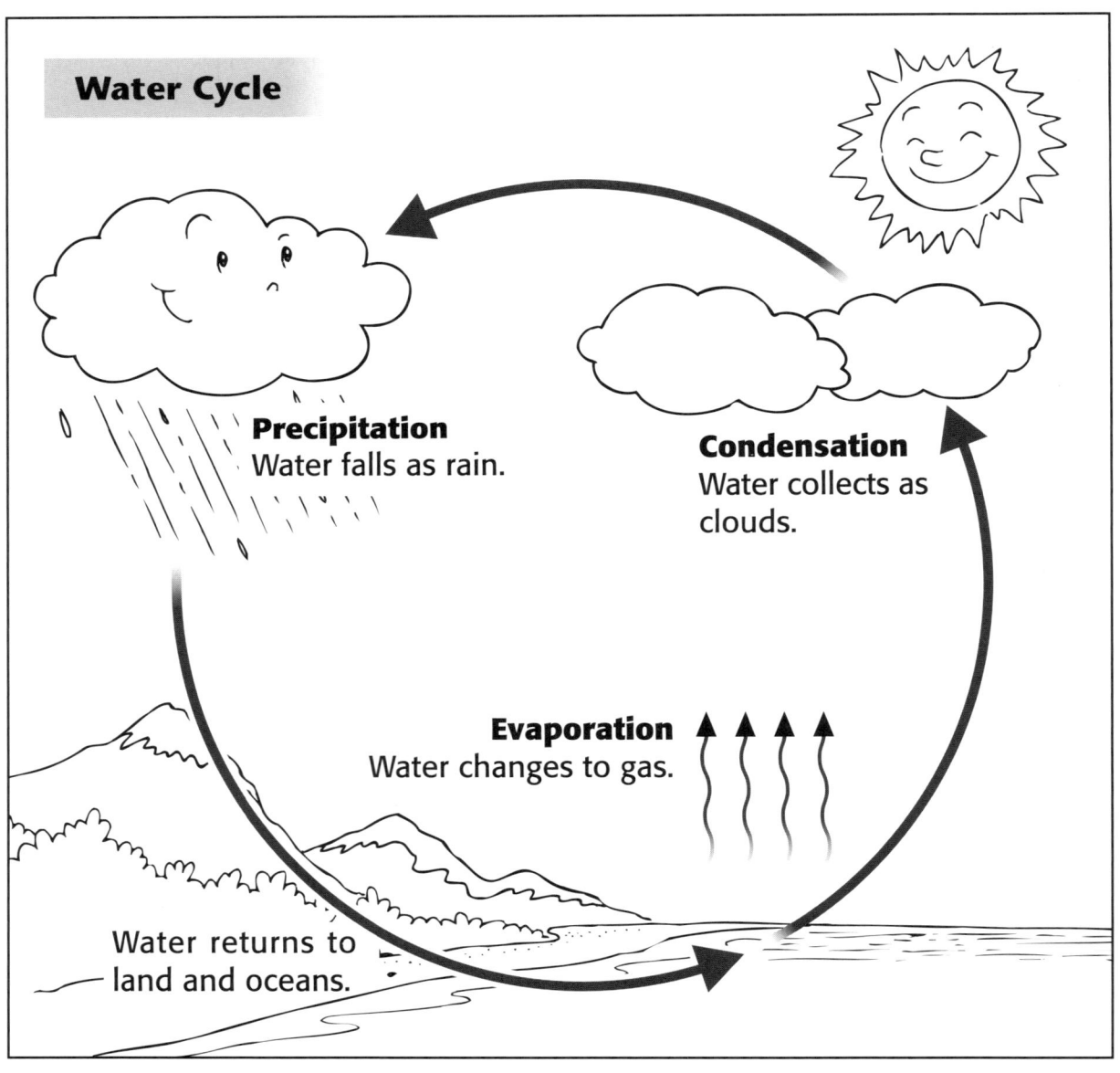

Water Cycle

Colour the various forms of water.

Water Cycle

Write the form of water each picture shows.

solid   liquid   gas

1.

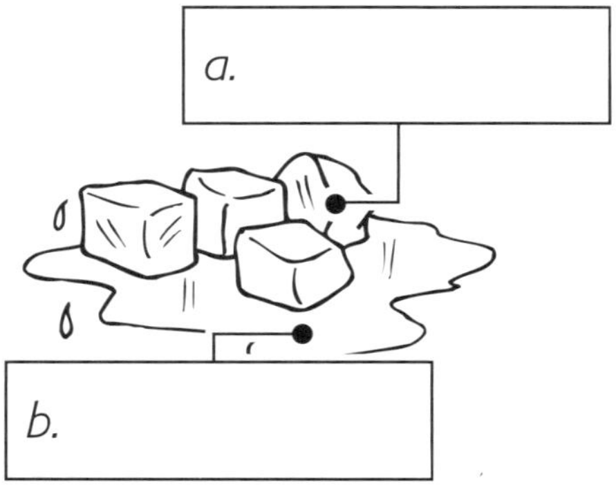

a. _____

b. _____

2.

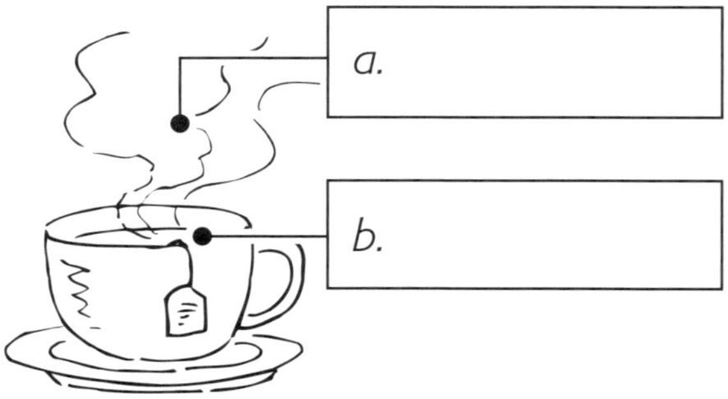

a. _____

b. _____

3.

_____

4.

_____

5.

_____

6.

_____

Water Cycle

Match the words with the correct descriptions. Then label the diagram with the words.

1.

Condensation •

Evaporation •

Precipitation •

Descriptions

• Water falls as rain.

• Water changes to gas.

• Water collects as clouds.

2.

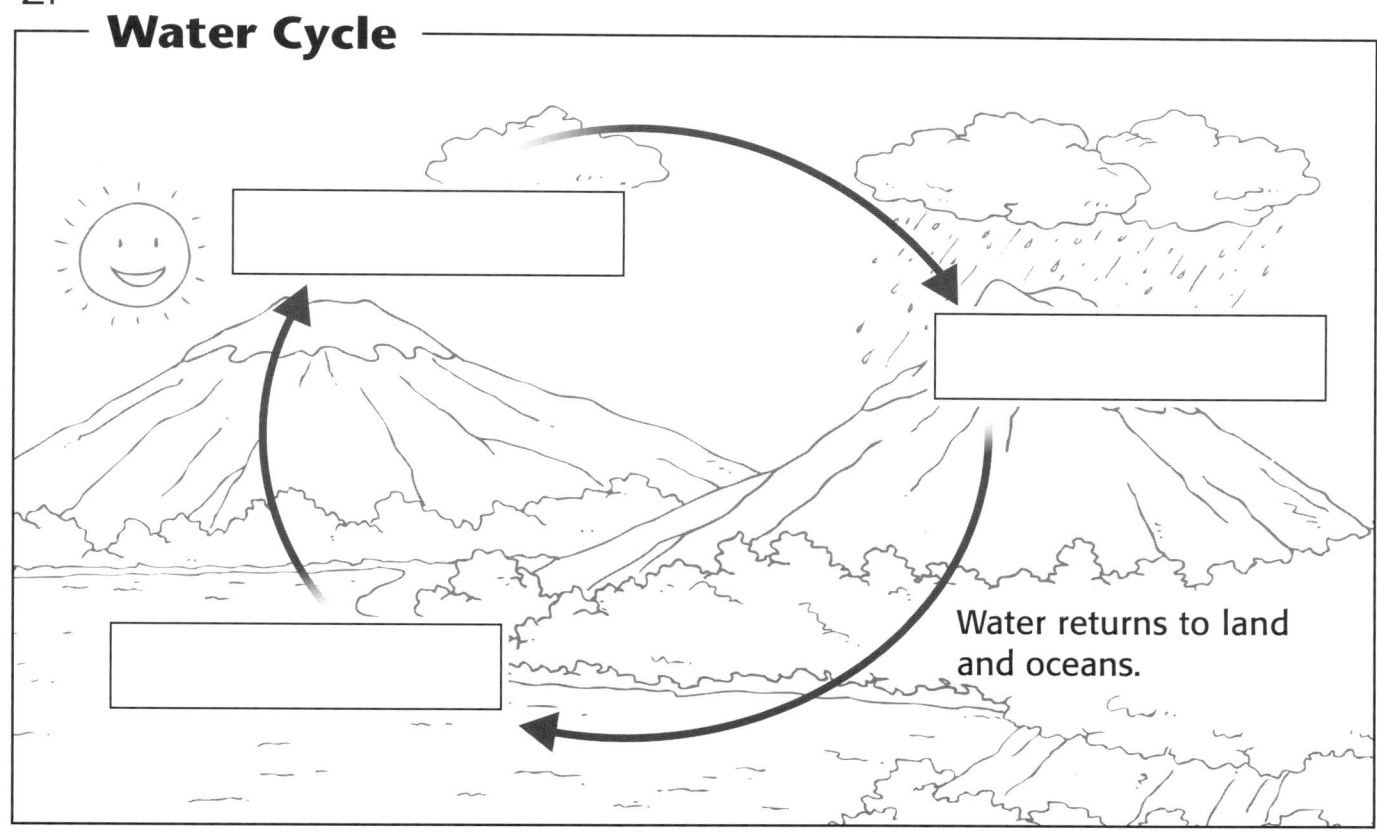

Water Cycle

Water returns to land and oceans.

Weather and Climate

Weather is what is happening in a place at a given time. It is what we hear about on the television news every day. Weather changes from day to day or even hour to hour. For example, it may rain for an hour and then become sunny and clear.   Weather includes daily changes in precipitation, such as rain and snow, temperatures, and wind conditions. What is the weather like today?

The temperature is 25 °C today.

Climate is a big picture of weather in a place over many years. This includes average weather conditions, regular weather sequences (like spring, summer, fall, and winter) and special weather events (like floods and hurricanes). Climate tells us what it is usually like in a place. For example, the Northwest Territories and Nunavut are known as having an arctic climate, while Halifax has a humid climate with warm summers and cold winters. How would you describe the climate where you live?

It's so much fun to ski in winter!

Weather and Climate

Tell whether the sentences are about "weather" or "climate".

1. It is cloudy and windy today.   _____

2. Mr. Cowan wonders why there is a hail storm in this season.   _____

3. Uncle Jason is living in a warm and humid city.   _____

4. The highest temperature will be around 32°C tomorrow.   _____

5. Mr. Wood needs to buy a down jacket because he will stay in that cold city for three months.   _____

6. Judy puts on her waterproof windbreaker and carries an umbrella to get ready for the coming storm.   _____

7.  *Although it's hot and dry here, it's a good place to live and play in.*

_____

Weather and Climate

Which months fall in each season? Write them on the line. Then draw a picture to go with each season.

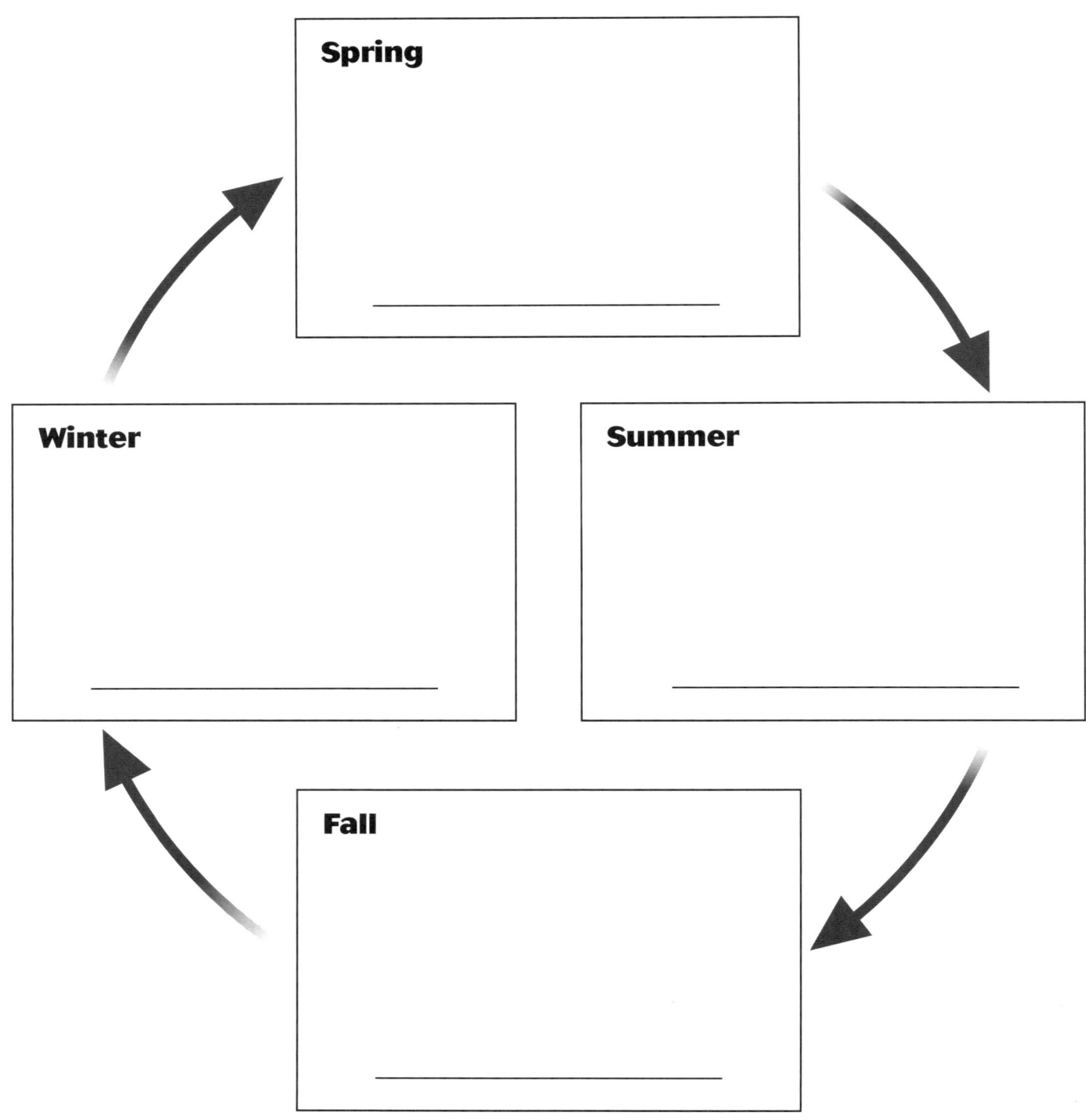

Weather and Climate

What is the weather like this week? Colour the thermometer to show the highest temperature and then colour the "weather picture" for each day.

Sun	Mon	Tue	Wed	Thu	Fri	Sat
°C	°C	°C	°C	°C	°C	°C

Food Chains

All living things depend on one another to live. A food chain shows how each living thing gets its food. Some animals eat plants and some animals eat other animals. A food chain always starts with plant life and ends with an animal.

A food chain consists of three main parts:

- The **sun** provides the energy for everything on Earth.

- Plants are called **producers**. They are able to use light energy from the sun to make their own food.

- Animals that eat plants and/or other animals are called **consumers**. There are three types of consumers:

  - Animals that eat only plants are called **herbivores**.

  - Animals that eat other animals are called **carnivores**.

  - Animals that eat both animals and plants are called **omnivores**.

In a food chain, energy is passed from one link to another. If there is a broken link in a food chain, some animals may not survive. So, it is important to keep the population of plants and animals in balance.

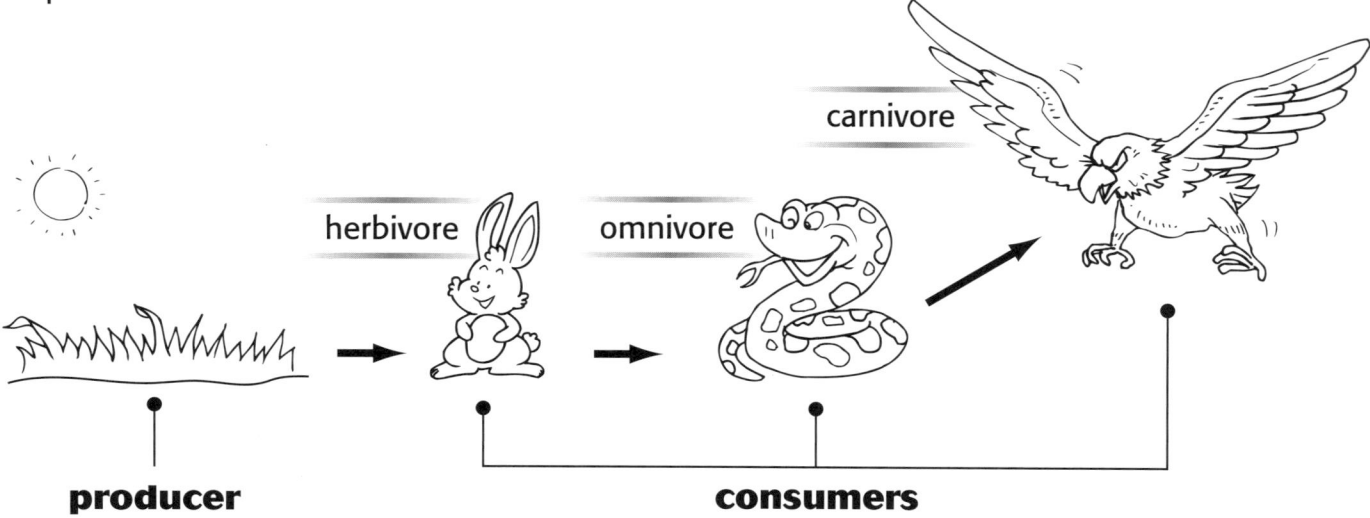

carnivore

herbivore   omnivore

producer   **consumers**

Food Chains

Fill in the blanks to complete the sentences.

producers	herbivores	omnivores	consumers
food chains	plants	carnivores	sun

1. Living things connect to one another by _____ .

2. Plants get energy from the _____ to live and grow.

3. _____ have the ability to make their food by using the energy from the sun.

4. _____ are the animals that never eat other animals.

5. Animals that eat other animals are called _____ .

6. A food chain consists of three main parts: _____ , _____ , and _____ .

7. The favourite food of black bears are nuts, acorns, and insects. Black bears are _____ .

Food Chains

Draw arrows to show a food chain. Then colour the producers green and the consumers red.

Food Chains

Cut out the pictures and glue them in the correct places to complete the food chain. Then answer the questions.

1. A Food Chain

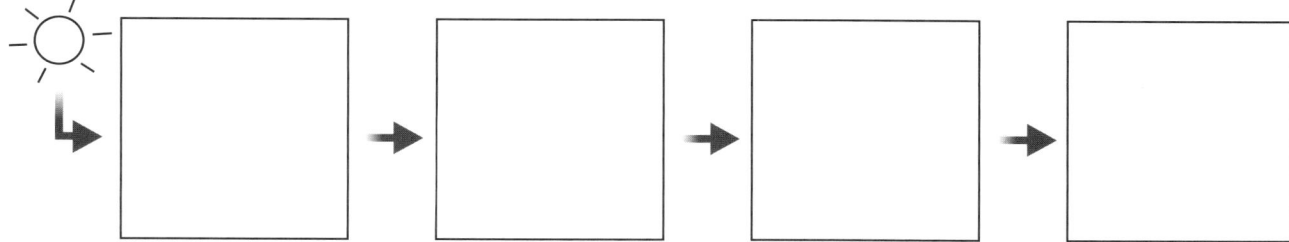

2. What would happen if the plants were removed from the chain?

   A   The animals would be healthier.

   B   The animals would not survive.

3. What would happen if the ants were removed from the chain?

   A   The spiders would starve to death.

   B   The population of sparrows would increase.

- ✂

Checklist: Our Natural World

❏   I understand the meaning of "atmosphere".

❏   I know what the greenhouse effect is.

❏   I know the importance of our atmosphere.

❏   I understand the water cycle.

❏   I can identify different forms of water.

❏   I can describe each process in the water cycle.

❏   I know the difference between weather and climate.

❏   I can identify the four seasons.

❏   I can use pictures to tell weather.

❏   I know how to tell temperatures with a thermometer.

❏   I understand what food chains mean.

❏   I can identify the main parts of a food chain.

❏   I am able to use pictures to show food chains.

❏   I know the importance of each part of the food chain.

Global Warming **1-3**
Grades

Causes of Global Warming

Global Warming

Global warming is the warming of the world's weather, caused by the increase of greenhouse gases in the air that trap the sun's heat. These gases, including carbon dioxide, are given off by burning fossil fuels and destroying rainforests.

Fossil fuels are burned in power stations to make electricity. The cutting down of forests also contributes to the rising levels of carbon dioxide because a huge amount of carbon dioxide is produced when trees are burned. Moreover, there will be fewer trees to absorb carbon dioxide.

If global warming continues, there will be changes in climate. Violent storms are becoming more common throughout the world. Heat waves, droughts, and floods occur more often too. Animals and plants may not be able to survive in this wild weather.

We have already caused damage to our atmosphere. What can we do now to repair our damaged Earth and protect it from further damage?

Global Warming

Put a check mark ✔ in the circle if the sentence is correct; otherwise, put a cross ✗.

1. Global warming means to the rise in the average temperature of the Earth.   ◯

2. During the burning of fossil fuels, no carbon dioxide is emitted.   ◯

3. Global warming does not affect living things on Earth.   ◯

4. Trees help reduce the amount of carbon dioxide.   ◯

5. If the warming gets worse, there may be more storms and floods.   ◯

Answer the questions.

6. What are the main sources of carbon dioxide?

    _____

    _____

7. What will happen if global warming continues?

    _____

    _____

Global Warming

Colour the parts that show the emissions of carbon dioxide.

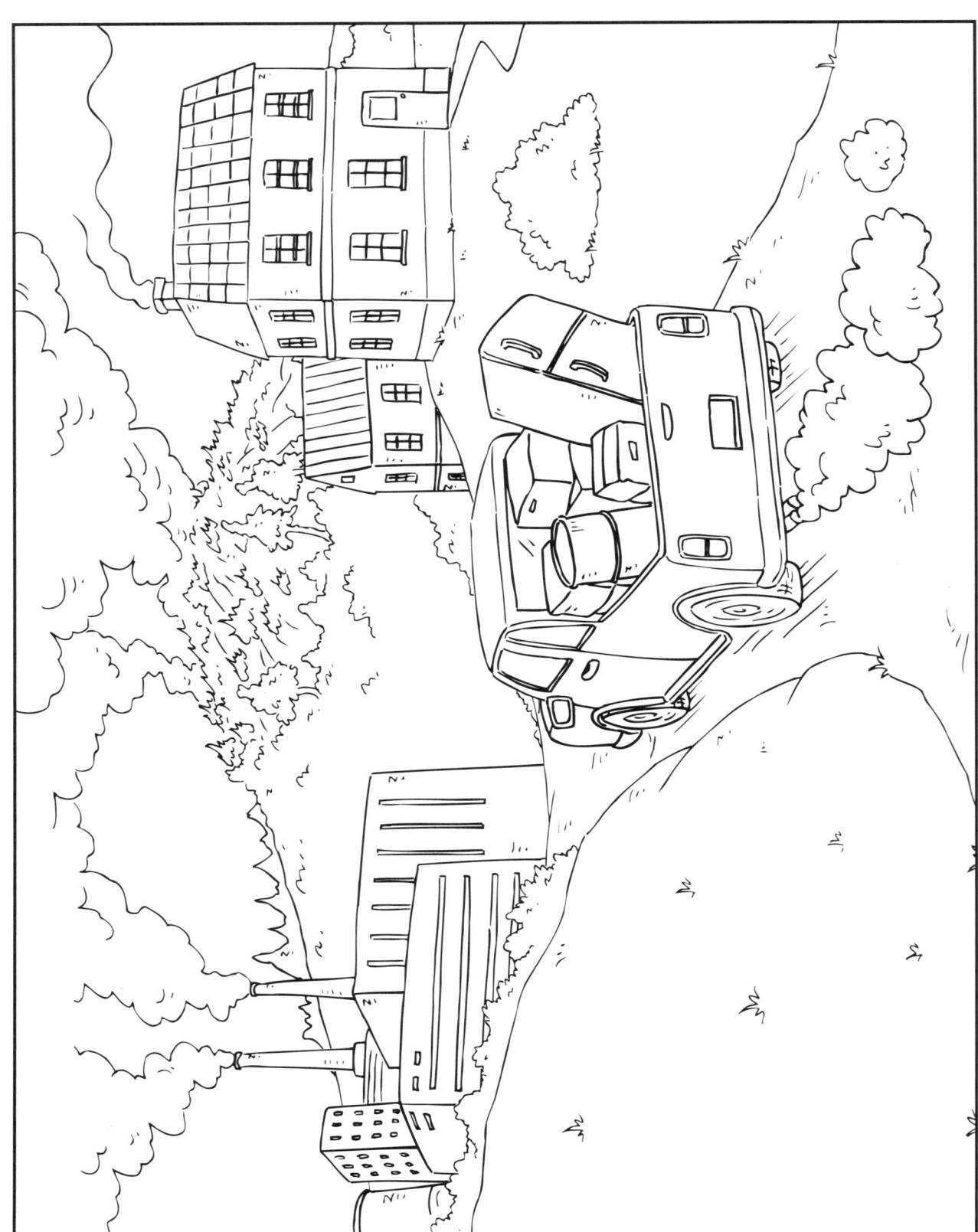

Global Warming

Glue the "carbon dioxide" (CO_2) cutouts in the atmosphere to complete the poster.

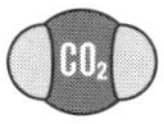

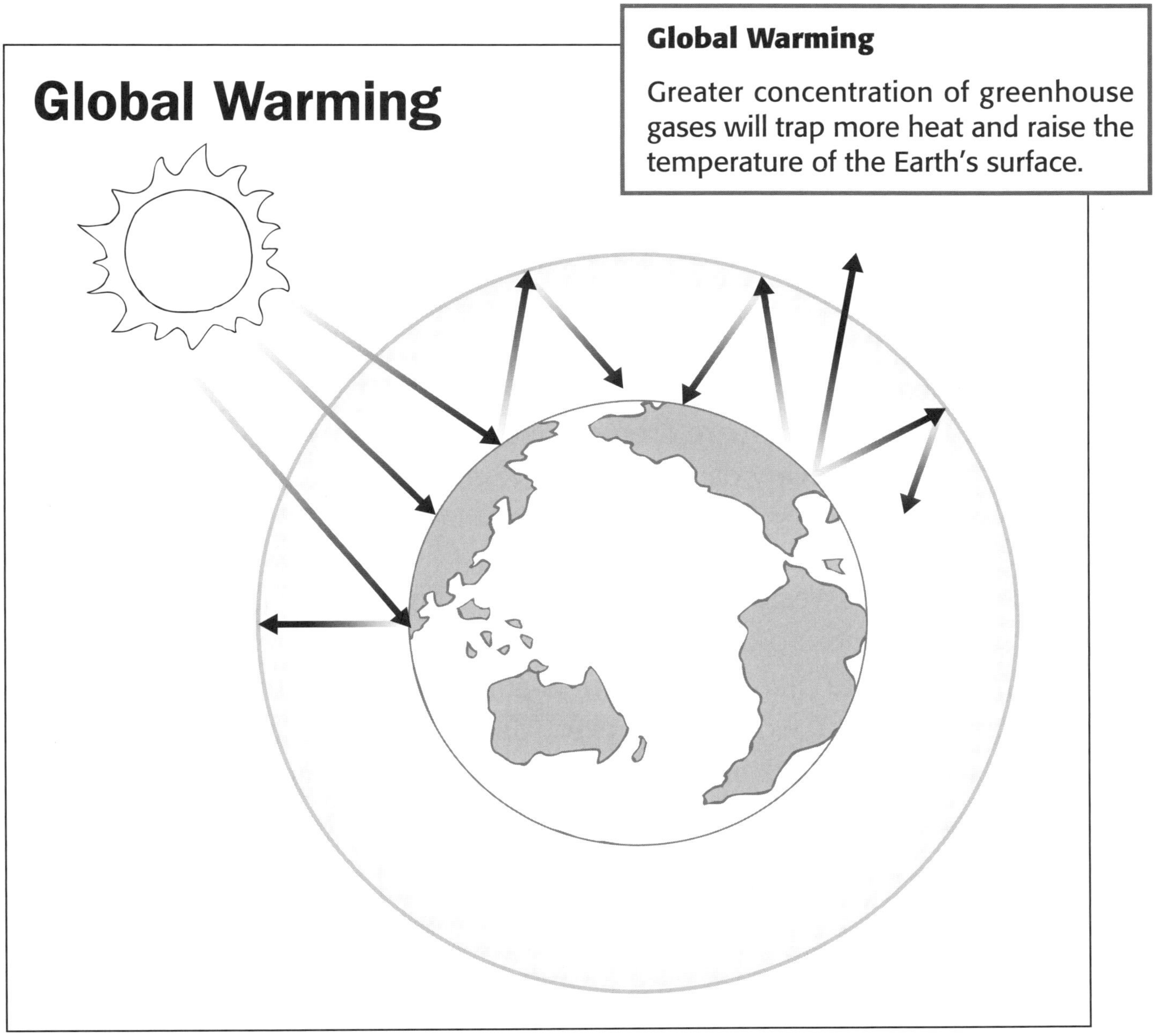

Global Warming

Global Warming

Greater concentration of greenhouse gases will trap more heat and raise the temperature of the Earth's surface.

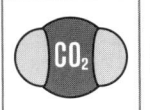  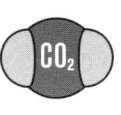 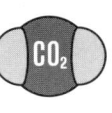     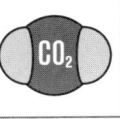 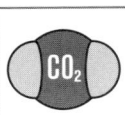

Pollution

The whole world that we live in is our **environment**. It includes the air we breathe, the water we drink, and the land that we live on. Our environment provides us with different natural resources, such as fuels and lumber, for our survival.

However, the things that we put back into our environment are often harmful. Factories create many poisonous waste products that go into the air and oceans. Farmers use chemicals and fertilizers that are then carried into rivers by rain. We also create huge amounts of trash every day. Anything we put back into the environment that harms it or makes it dirty is called **pollution**.

All pollution is waste. Waste is discarded material and when it is released into the environment, it becomes pollution. It may harm our health and cause damage to the world around us – the plants and animals and the habitats they live in. As the number of people in the world grows every day, air pollution, water pollution, and land pollution problems will become more and more serious if we do not handle them properly.

Pollution

Check ✔ the pictures that show pollution.

1.
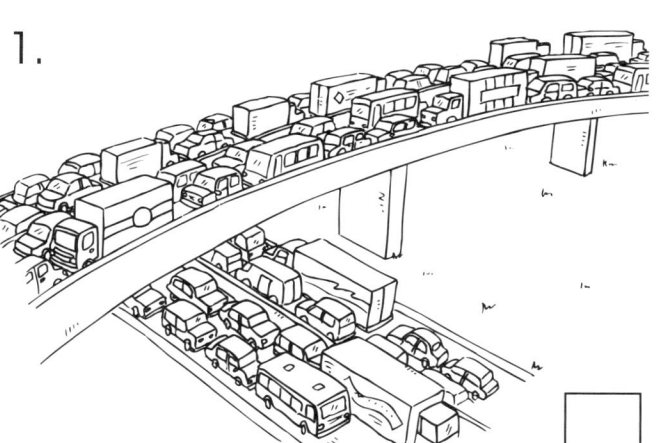

2.

3.

4.

5.

6.

        Global Warming | G.1-3

Pollution

Fill in the blanks.

air   pollution   water   land   environment   fuels   waste

1. _____ is the damage we cause to the world we live on.

2. There are various types of pollution including _____ pollution, _____ pollution, and _____ pollution.

3. The _____ is the whole world we live in.

4. As the world's population is growing, the amount of _____ produced increases dramatically which intensifies land pollution.

5. _____ are among the natural resources that humans use for survival.

Answer the questions.

6. What is the environment?

   _____

   _____

7. What is pollution?

   _____

   _____

Pollution

Complete the poster of "Pollution".

- poisonous fumes from factories
- wood for houses
- coal for energy
- garbage from people
- water for drinking
- chemicals from farms

Pollution

Things We Take from Earth

Things We Put Back into Earth

Earth

Different Kinds of Pollution

The three main kinds of pollution that have the greatest impact on Earth: air pollution, water pollution, and land pollution.

Air Pollution

Smoke from fires, dust from building sites, gas fumes from stoves, gases and toxic chemicals from factories, and gases from car engines cause air pollution. The released gases, such as carbon dioxide and methane, intensify the effect of global warming. Moreover, air pollution can make it difficult for us to breathe and can cause cancer and other diseases.

Gases from factories intensify the effect of global warming.

Water Pollution

When harmful substances such as oil and chemical wastes enter the water, water pollution results. Oil is the most damaging form of water pollution because it harms wildlife.

Land Pollution

Waste is garbage. Much waste is buried in landfills. Some is burned, causing air pollution. Hazardous waste is harmful to people and the environment. The more garbage we produce, the more resources and space we will need to dispose of it. Running out of space to locate landfill sites is a big problem.

Different Kinds of Pollution

Look at each picture. Then tell what kind of pollution it might cause.
Write "air pollution", "water pollution", or "land pollution" on the line.

1.

_____

2.

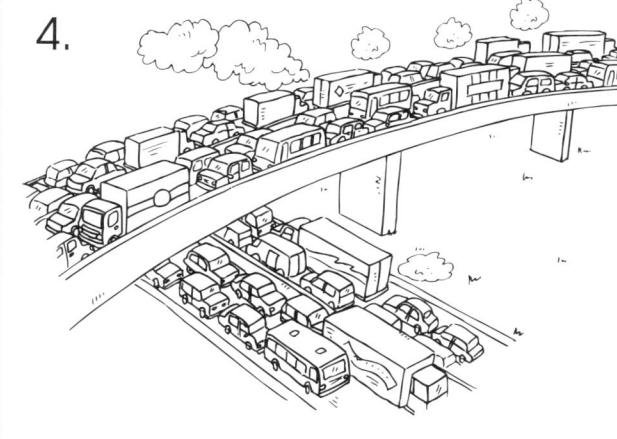

_____

3.

_____

4.

_____

5.

_____

Different Kinds of Pollution

Write "air pollution", "water pollution", or "land pollution" on the line to match the description of each child.

1. Leon says, "Waste from livestock farms is dumped into the waterways. It puts our health at risk."

    _____

2. Sally says, "Don't you know that our homes let out toxic fumes when fuels are burned?"

    _____

3. Kevin says, "Animals may die if they swallow garbage like plastic bags."

    _____

4.

    I know that pesticides can prevent insects from eating crops, but they can be dangerous when they are washed into rivers.

    _____

5.

    This problem seems to be more serious in richer countries because people living there use more cars which give off a mix of polluting gases.

    _____

6.

    If this landfill site cannot hold any more garbage, where should we dispose of the garbage then?

    _____

Different Kinds of Pollution

Record the kinds and the amount of waste you produce in the next two days. Then answer the question.

	Item (waste)	Quantity
Day 1		
Day 2		

Do you think you are one of the people who cause land pollution?

Item (waste)	Quantity
plastic bag	3

_____

Checklist: Causes of Global Warming

❏   I know the effect of global warming on Earth.

❏   I know the cause of global warming.

❏   I understand that global warming leads to climate change.

❏   I can complete a diagram to show how greenhouse gases trap heat and raise the average Earth's temperature.

❏   I know the meaning of pollution.

❏   I understand that the huge amounts of waste we create will harm our environment.

❏   I know pollution problems are getting worse.

❏   I can identify pictures showing pollution.

❏   I can complete a diagram to show the things we take from Earth and the things we put back into Earth.

❏   I know there are three main kinds of pollution: air pollution, water pollution, and land pollution.

❏   I can tell the causes of air pollution, water pollution, and land pollution.

❏   I can identify different kinds of pollution.

❏   I can record the amount of waste I produced on a chart.

36   Global Warming | G.1-3

Effects of
Global Warming

Unusual Weather

Many scientists believe that the changes in weather are due to global warming. Some areas in the world are becoming drier and some are becoming wetter. These changes bring us lots of unexpected disasters.

More Hurricanes

Hurricanes are powerful storms that form over warm oceans. As the average temperature of the Earth is rising, oceans are getting warmer and warmer. As a result, storms gather more heat energy and become more violent and more frequent.

More Floods and Droughts

Global warming changes precipitation patterns. Floods and droughts become more common. Warmer temperatures make some farming areas too dry to grow crops, and some places are in danger of turning into deserts. On the other hand, some places on Earth may have heavy rainstorms.

More Wildfires

Higher temperatures and greater evaporation also lead to larger and more devastating wildfires. These fires cause massive loss of plant life and lots of damage. To make things worse, huge amounts of carbon dioxide are released into the atmosphere and intensify the greenhouse effect.

Huge amount of carbon dioxide is released when plants are burned.

Unusual Weather

Match the words with the correct descriptions.

Hurricanes   Floods   Droughts   Wildfires

1. During heavy rains, when rivers overflow or ocean waves come onshore, these may happen.   _____

2. These are powerful tropical storms that bring strong winds and heavy rain.   _____

3. Some places are without rain for a long period.   _____

4. These are dangerous for people living in forests and wooded areas. They might be caused by lightning and they burn large areas.   _____

Answer the questions.

5. What may cause wildfires?

_____

6. Where do hurricanes form? Where does their energy come from?

_____

Unusual Weather

Cut out a picture of a disaster related to global warming from a newspaper or an old magazine. Glue it in the box. Then write sentences to describe the disaster.

Don't forget to give your picture a title.

Description: _____

_____

_____

_____

Unusual Weather

Look at the excerpts from some articles. Write "Droughts", "Floods", "Wildfires", or "Hurricanes" to tell what the articles are about.

The average rainfall in the south of the Sahara Desert in Africa has dropped. Most of the water holes there can no longer provide water for cattle or crops.

1. _____

In 2007, massive floods struck the southern Mexican states. Lots of places were under water and about one million residents were affected by the floods.

3. _____

In 1993, the Mississippi River flooded a huge area of land.

2. _____

Wildfires raged across Southern California in late October 2003. They caused the death of more than 20 people, including a firefighter.

5. _____

Hurricane Katrina formed on August 25, 2005. It caused severe damage along the Gulf Coast, devastating the Mississippi cities.

4. _____

There is a growing risk of forest fires in Yellowstone National Park in the United States. Its summer temperatures are getting higher and higher every year.

6. _____

Rising Sea Levels

Sea levels are affected by global warming in two ways. First, when seas get warmer due to global warming, the water expands and sea levels rise. Second, warmer temperatures melt the ice in the polar regions. The melting ice flows into the seas. As a result, sea levels rise.

The rise of sea levels is a major problem for people who live on low-lying coastal plains and small islands because these places are threatened with floods. If coasts flood, millions of people worldwide will be made homeless. Small islands or large areas of low and flat countries, such as Bangladesh and the Netherlands, may end up underwater.

If global warming continues, more homes and lands will end up underwater.

Apart from severe flooding, higher sea levels will also cause a series of problems such as erosion of beaches, loss of wetlands, and destruction of farmland.

No one knows to what extent sea levels will rise in the future, but there is one thing we are sure about – if global warming continues, one day many islands will submerge in oceans and thousands of people will lose their homes or even their lives.

Rising Sea Levels

Circle the correct answers.

1. How does global warming affect sea levels?

    A. Sea levels rise.   B. Sea levels fall.
    C. Sea levels remain the same.

2. Why does the ice in the polar regions melt?

    A. Sea levels rise.
    B. Warmer temperatures melt it.
    C. Polar regions are threatened with people.

3. Why is the rise of sea levels a problem to coasts and small islands?

    A. Travelling by sea will be less convenient.
    B. People cannot do water activities.
    C. There will be more floods.

4. What problems are caused by higher sea levels?

    A. Erosion of beaches   B. Severe flooding
    C. Farming   D. Emissions of carbon dioxide

5. What will happen if global warming continues?

    A. Sea levels will be lower and lower.
    B. Many islands will submerge in oceans.
    C. Many people will be made homeless.
    D. Floods will become weaker and less frequent.

Rising Sea Levels

Look at the pictures that show the same place in different years. Cut out the correct houses and glue them onto the pictures. Colour the water blue to show the sea levels.

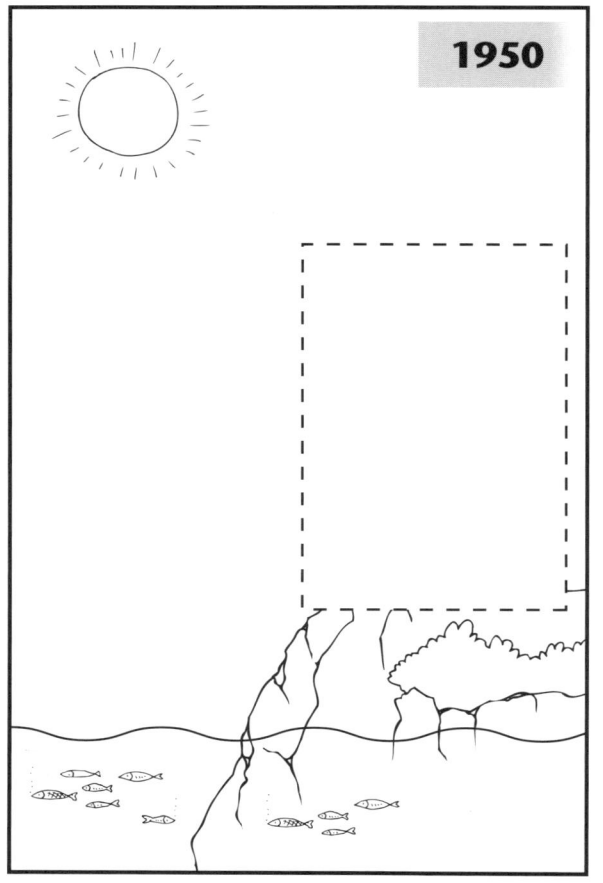

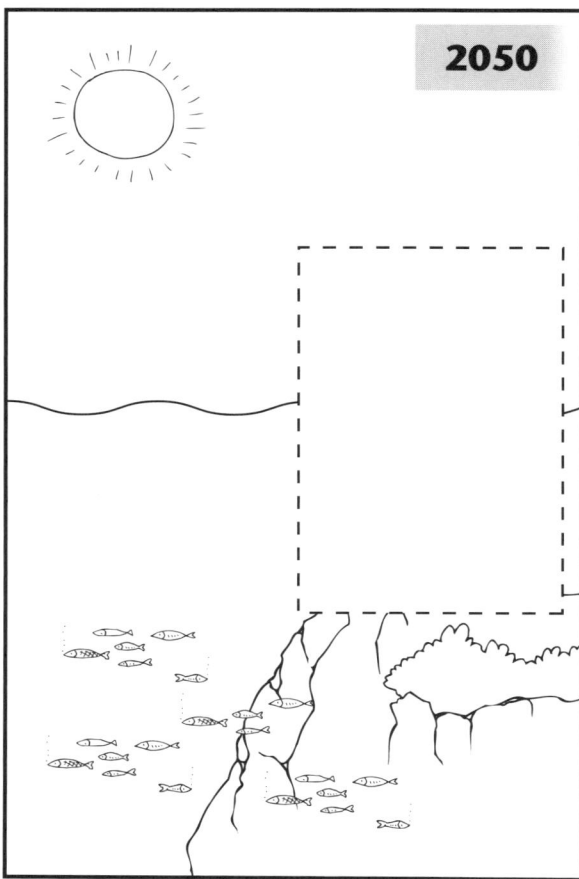

Name: _____   **Date:** _____

Rising Sea Levels

Fill in the blanks to complete the map.

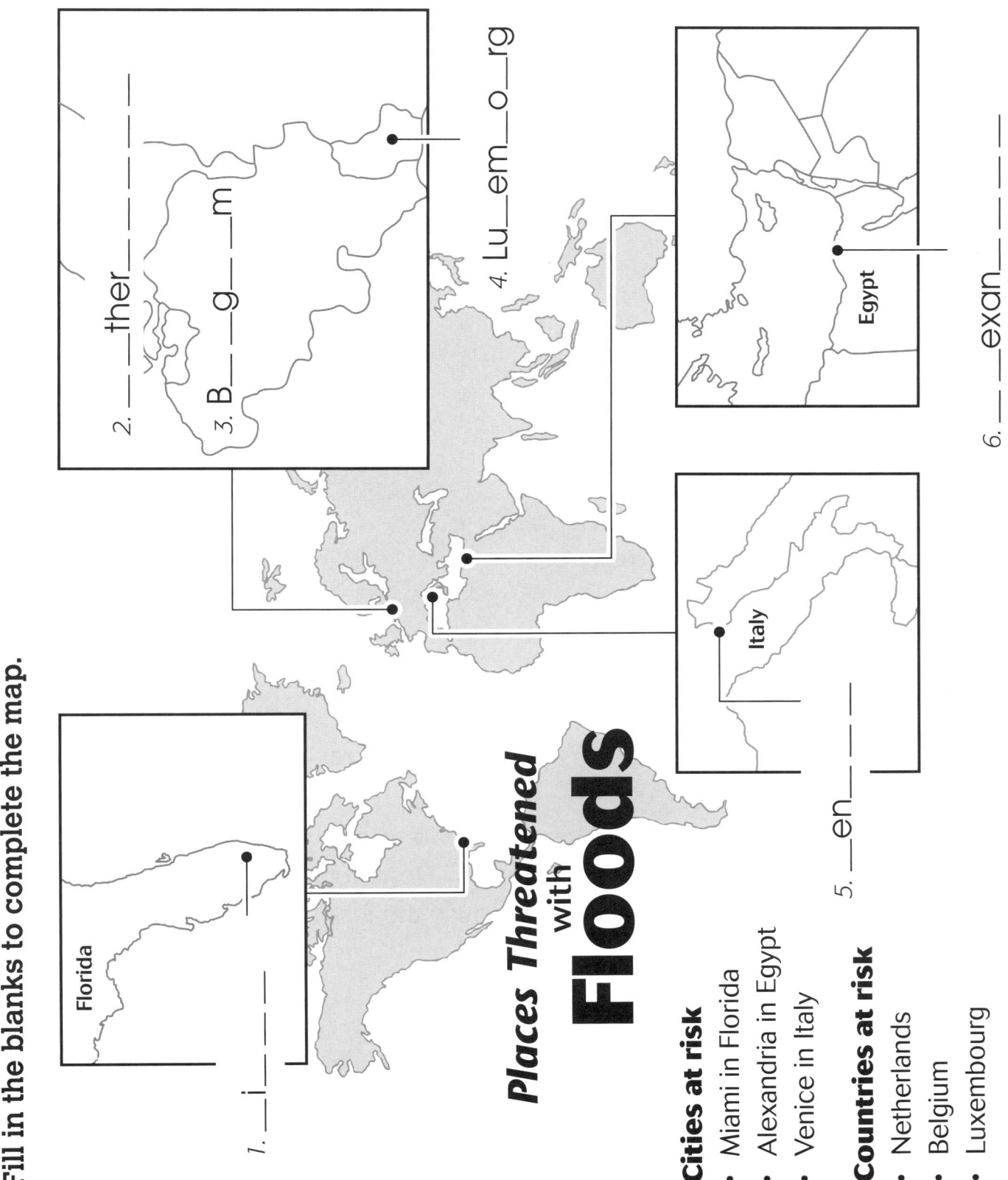

2. ___ ___ ther ___ ___ ___ ___

3. B ___ ___ g ___ ___ m

4. Lu ___ em ___ o ___ rg

6. ___ ___ exan ___ ___ ___ ___

5. ___ en ___ ___ ___

1. ___ i ___ ___ ___ ___

Florida

Egypt

Italy

Places Threatened

with

Floods

Cities at risk
- Miami in Florida
- Alexandria in Egypt
- Venice in Italy

Countries at risk
- Netherlands
- Belgium
- Luxembourg

Animals and Plants in Danger

Changes in climate can affect the way ecosystems work and upset the habitats of living things. In the past, climate changes occurred slowly, allowing animals and plants to adapt to the new environment or move somewhere else. However, if future climate changes occur rapidly, animals and plants may not be able to react fast enough to survive. Here are some examples of animals and plants that are suffering from global warming.

Polar bears are drastically affected by climate change. Because of shorter winters, less ice cover, and less food available, female polar bears are unable to put on as much fat as possible in winter. Less fat on their bodies means fewer cubs are born, and those that are born are thin and weak. As a result, polar bears may face extinction.

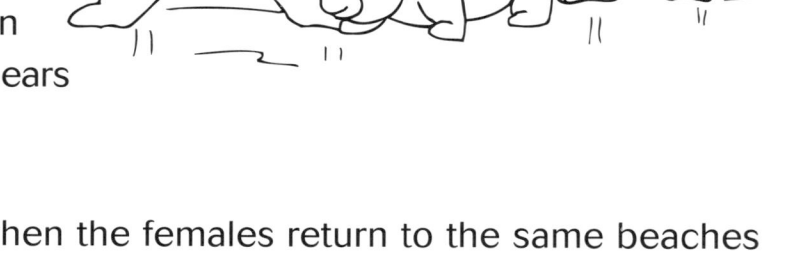

Sea turtles live at sea – except when the females return to the same beaches where they hatched to lay their eggs. Unfortunately, rising sea levels have made some of the beaches disappear. This puts sea turtles at a high risk of extinction.

Alpine plants are sensitive to warm temperatures. A study found that alpine plants are moving upwards to cooler regions. However, the farthest they can go is the mountain peak. Warm temperatures cause the loss of many alpine plants.

Animals and Plants in Danger

Check ✔ the correct sentences to tell how global warming causes some living things to face extinction.

1.

A Polar bears fail to reproduce strong and healthy offspring.

B Polar bears become more and more picky.

C Wintertime is getting longer.

2.

A Sea turtles make friends with whales.

B Rising sea levels cause sea turtles to lose their beaches for reproduction.

C Sea turtles cannot find food to eat.

3.

A Alpine plants are threatened by floods.

B Many people pick alpine plants.

C Warm temperatures force alpine plants to move upwards, and many die because of this.

Animals and Plants in Danger

Complete the poster to help people learn about the endangered polar bears.

Endangered Polar Bears — seals food reproduce fat melt

As the Earth's temperature becomes warmer, huge sheets of ice in the Arctic _1._____ . So, polar bears cannot travel across them to find and catch _2._____ and other prey. Without adequate _3._____ , polar bears cannot gain the _4._____ they need to survive the long winter. In addition, it is hard for polar bears with less fat to _5._____ strong and healthy cubs.

Don't you think we need to do something to protect polar bears?

Animals and Plants in Danger

Read what Gary says.
Answer the questions.

Global warming causes the ice around Antarctica to melt and break apart. This melting is dangerous to emperor penguins because they breed on huge sheets of ice. They breed far from the edges of the ice, so their chicks will be kept a distance from the ocean. If the ice breaks before the chicks hatch, the chicks may fall into the ocean and drown or freeze to death.

1. What causes the ice around Antarctica to melt?

   _____

   _____

2. Where do emperor penguins breed?

   _____

   _____

3. What will happen if the ice breaks before the chicks hatch?

   _____

   _____

Threats to Humans

Climate change caused by global warming affects all living things on Earth, including humans. The slight rise in temperatures has already made humans suffer a lot.

Droughts

Based on a stable climate system, humans can develop agricultural systems to plan what crops to plant or what size of livestock to feed at particular times of the year. Due to the change in climate, droughts make crops fail and livestock die. As a result, a series of problems happen, such as extensive damage to plants, reduction in food production, death of livestock, and people starving.

A ship is left on a land that was once covered with water.

Heat Waves

A heat wave is a period of abnormally and uncomfortably hot and often humid weather, usually lasting from a few days to over a week. Heat waves are dangerous because they cause illnesses such as heat strokes and heat rashes, which threaten our lives. In the disastrous heat wave of 2003 in Europe, more than 20 000 people died from heat-related illnesses. With continued global warming, the intensity and duration of heat waves seem likely to increase. Can you imagine how many more people will become casualties in future heat waves?

Threats to Humans

Check ✔ the correct sentences and cross out ✘ the incorrect ones.

1. Global warming does not affect the lives of humans. ⭕

2. Droughts damage the growth of crops. ⭕

3. Humans can plant whatever crops they prefer in a particular area. ⭕

4. A heat wave may last about 3 to 10 days. ⭕

5. A lot of people die every year because of heat waves. ⭕

Answer the questions.

6. What are the problems caused by droughts?

_____

_____

7. What is a heat wave?

_____

_____

8. What kinds of illnesses are related to heat?

_____

_____

Threats to Humans

Colour the pictures that show droughts.

1.

2.

3.

4.

5.

6.

Threats to Humans

Read what Thomas says. Help him complete the table. Then answer the questions.

> *Toronto Public Health monitors the weather every day from May 15 to September 31 every year. It alerts those people most at risk of heat-related illnesses by issuing heat alerts. It issued 3 heat alerts in 2003, 2 in 2004, 8 in 2005, 9 in 2006, and 10 in 2007.*

1.

Year	Number of Heat Alerts Issued
2003	
2004	
2005	
2006	
2007	

2. Which government department issues heat alerts?

_____

3. What can you tell by the number of heat alerts issued between 2003 and 2007? Would the number of heat alerts be greater than 10 in 2015?

_____

Checklist: Effects of Global Warming

❏   I know that global warming is the cause of unusual weather.

❏   I know the causes of hurricanes, floods, droughts, and wildfires.

❏   I can find news about disasters related to global warming.

❏   I can identify different kinds of disasters.

❏   I know that global warming leads to rising sea levels.

❏   I understand that the rise of sea levels threatens the lives of people and causes lots of problems.

❏   I can complete a map to show places in the world threatened with floods.

❏   I know that polar bears, sea turtles, and alpine plants are endangered living things.

❏   I know how global warming makes polar bears, sea turtles, penguins, and alpine plants face extinction.

❏   I know that droughts are serious problems to humans.

❏   I understand that heat waves can cause a series of fatal heat-related illnesses in humans.

❏   I know that there is a growing trend of heat waves.

Global Warming
Grades **1-3**

Save the Earth

Things People Are Doing to Save the Earth

There is no doubt that lots of human activities, such as burning of fossil fuels to generate electricity or power vehicles, release huge amounts of greenhouse gases. However, scientists and many other people are now working together to tackle these problems and find ways to control the damage.

Alternative Energy Sources

- Renewable energy such as sun energy, wind energy, and water energy are energies that never runs out. Solar panels, wind farms, and hydroelectric power stations are built to generate electricity. These renewable energies do not emit carbon dioxide and the demand for fossil fuels is reduced.

- Cow dung and rotting waste can be used as fuels. As they rot, they release a gas called biogas that can be used for cooking and heating. In addition, using rotting waste helps reduce the amount of garbage.

Recycling

- Most towns and cities have recycling schemes. Glass, cans, paper, and some plastics can be recycled and reused. Recycling can help reduce the consumption of natural resources.

- Recycling can save energy because it takes less energy to recycle materials than to make them from scratch.

Things People Are Doing to Save the Earth

Match each description with the correct energy source. Then name the source shown in each picture.

(A) Hydroelectric power station   (B) Solar energy

(C) Wind farm   (D) Biogas

◯ Rotting waste and dung produce this gas which can be used for cooking.

◯ This is the energy from the sun. We use solar panels to change sunlight into electricity.

◯ We use wind to spin a propeller that is hooked to a generator to produce electricity.

◯ Tides can turn turbines under water. This is a renewable source of energy that can generate electricity.

Things People Are Doing to Save the Earth

Trace the "Recycle" sign and colour the recycling box blue. Then write sentences to encourage people to recycle.

Recycle

Things People Are Doing to Save the Earth

Fill in the blanks to complete the steps taken to recycle glass. Then number the pictures 1 – 3.

bottles   crushed   heated

Steps Taken to Recycle Glass

1. Glass bottles are sorted, cleaned, and _____ .

2. The crushed glass is _____ till it melts.

3. The hot glass is shaped into new _____ .

Things We Can Do to Save the Earth

We can do a lot to help slow down global warming. If everyone uses natural resources such as water, trees, and land wisely, it can help reduce the amount of waste and the emission of carbon dioxide. Take a look at the things that we can do.

At Home

- Put recycle items such as aluminum cans, newspapers, and plastic bottles into the recycling bin.
- Turn off things that use electricity when you are not using them.
- Use cloth napkins instead of paper napkins.
- When you brush your teeth, remember to turn off the faucet. Never let the water run.
- Take a quick shower or a shallow bath.
- Decide what you want before you open the refrigerator.
- On hot and sunny days, close shades and curtains to keep your home cool.

At School

- If you live near your school, you should walk or ride your bike to school.
- Turn off the lights when everyone leaves the classroom.
- Pack your lunch in containers that can be reused or recycled.
- Ask your teacher if you can write on both sides of a sheet of paper.
- Use crayons, rulers, and other school supplies until you really need new ones.
- Collect and reuse paper clips, thumbtacks, and elastic bands.

There are many things we can do to help save the world. Talk with your parents and teachers to see how much more we can do to use less.

Things We Can Do to Save the Earth

Check ✔ the things that we should do to save the Earth. Then give two suggestions.

Things We Should Do

1. ◯ When you take a bath in a tub, keep the water level low.

2. ◯ When you water your garden, just turn on the sprinkler and let the water run until it overflows.

3. ◯ Save plastic and cardboard packages for making crafts.

4. ◯ Turn off the television and video player when you have finished watching a movie.

5. ◯ When the air conditioner is on, you may leave the door open.

6. ◯ Save bows, ribbons, and boxes from gifts. Reuse them when needed.

7. ◯ Take your own shopping bags with you when going shopping.

8. ◯ Use paper plates and paper napkins for your birthday party.

9. ✔ _____

10. ✔ _____

Things We Can Do to Save the Earth

Put the recycle items into the correct boxes. Write the letters.

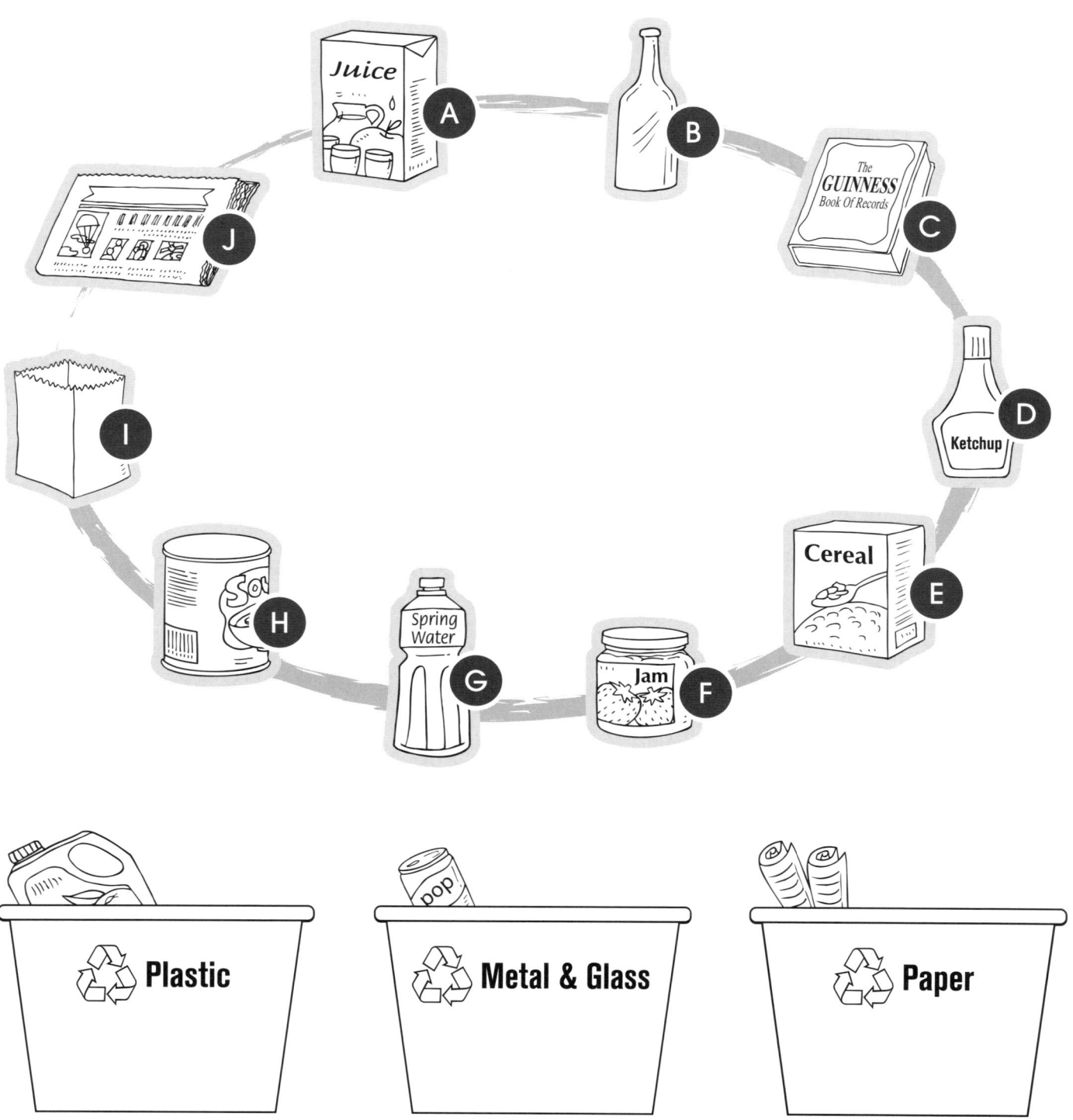

Things We Can Do to Save the Earth

Read what Sally says. Then colour the things that are made from recycled items.

Some slides and playground equipment are made from recycled plastic bottles. Some playgrounds have soft pads on the ground. Do you know what materials are used to make these soft pads? They are made from recycled tires.

Items made from recycled plastic bottles: **blue**

Items made from recycled car tires: **green**

Checklist: Save the Earth

❏   I know that many people in the world are working together to tackle climate problems.

❏   I know that there are alternative energy sources.

❏   I understand the meaning of renewable sources of energy.

❏   I can identify different kinds of renewable sources of energy.

❏   I know the importance of recycling.

❏   I understand the advantages of recycling.

❏   I know the steps taken to recycle glass.

❏   I know that there are lots of things we can do to save the Earth.

❏   I can recycle lots of items at home or at school.

❏   I know how to sort recycle items.

❏   I know that lots of things are made from recycled items.

64   Global Warming | G.1-3

Global Warming **Grades 1-3**

Useful Facts

Useful Facts:

Saving Endangered Animals

Many people around the world are taking actions to protect endangered animals. Look at the two successful cases below which show us what people have been doing to save the endangered animals.

Case 1: Whooping Crane

The whooping crane is one of the endangered species in North America. With its long neck and legs, a whooping crane can reach a height of 1.5 metres, making it the tallest bird on the continent. Its wingspan is about 2 metres. In the 1700s, the number of whooping cranes was about 1500. Because of the destruction of their habitat, their population declined to an all-time low of 15 in 1941.

Fortunately, through the intervention of the Canadian Wildlife Service and the U.S. Fish and Wildlife Service, the number of cranes has increased. The current population of whooping cranes is 140.

Case 2: California Condor

The California condor is the largest flying bird in North America. In 1987, they were almost extinct because people hunted them and some of them ate lead-poisoned animals accidentally. The wild population of California condors was about 20. Then people caught and captive-bred all the remaining birds at the Los Angeles Zoo and the San Diego Wild Animal Park. By 2005, there were about 100 California condors living in captivity and about the same number of California condors had been released to the wild as well.

In 1987, California condors were almost extinct with a population of about 20.

Useful Facts:
Oil Spills

Oil Spills

Oil spills are major environmental problems. Every year, huge amounts of oil are spilled accidentally into the oceans. As a result, thousands of sea animals and plants are killed, and important habitats such as marshes are wrecked.

Oil sticks bird feathers together, preventing the birds from flying. If the birds swallow or breathe in oil, they will be poisoned or their lungs will be damaged. Oil also sticks to the fur of sea lions, sea otters, and other sea mammals, so it cannot keep them warm. The oil also irritates their eyes and noses, and poisons them.

Marsh grasses, mangroves, and sea plants provide habitats where animals live, feed, and breed. When these plants are damaged or killed by oil spills, how will the sea animals be affected?

Cleaning Up Oil Spills

Trained response teams always get ready for tracking oil spill problems. When oil spills, the first thing that response teams do is to prevent the oil spill from spreading. First of all, they use floating booms as barriers to surround a slick. Then they use sponge-like materials called sorbents, including straw, woodchips, and foam, to soak up the oil. The response teams can use special boats called skimmers that work like giant vacuum cleaners to suck the oil off the water as well.

Because of the prompt action of response teams, the destruction of our environment is drastically reduced. We have to thank response teams and hope they can find more ways to clean up oil spills in order to minimize the harm caused by the spills.

Useful Facts:

Crops Stored in "Doomsday Vault"

Thousands of seeds, plants, and crop varieties from all continents were shipped to a seed bank located in an Arctic mountain near the town of Longyearbyen, Norway, which is about 1000 kilometres from the North Pole.

The nickname of the seed bank is "Doomsday Vault". The vault is built 122 m deep into the Arctic permafrost, so all the seeds in the vault are kept at a constant temperature of -18°C. In case we have a natural or man-made disaster, and a collection of seeds is destroyed in its natural habitat, there would remain an alternative source. Because of the protection of the vault, it is believed that the seeds can be kept safely frozen for at least 200 years. Some of the seeds will be able to live and grow for even thousands of years!

Structure of the Vault

The vault is protected by high walls of fortified concrete, an armoured door, and a sensor alarm, and is built 130 metres above the current sea level, which is high enough to stand the worst flood when the ice sheets melt entirely due to global warming. The vault consists of three cold chambers each measuring 27 m by 10 m. It has a total capacity of holding up to 4.5 million batches of seeds from all known varieties of our main food crops.

Because of the sturdy design, scientists believe that this vault can ensure the survival of the world's most important crop species.

Global Warming
Grades 1-3

Project Ideas

Project Ideas:
A Mini Water Cycle

Do this experiment to see how water goes through a cycle.

Materials

- a small clean yogurt cup
- a small zip-lock bag
- water
- tape

Steps

1. Put a small amount of water in the yogurt cup.
2. Put the cup in a small zip-lock bag and close the bag.
3. Tape the bag carefully to a window where the sunlight comes in.
4. Observe the bag every 2 hours and tell what happens.

Write your observation and explain.

_____

_____

_____

_____

_____

70   Global Warming | G.1-3

Project Ideas:
The Greenhouse Effect

We all know that the greenhouse gases make the Earth warmer by trapping energy in the atmosphere. You can try this experiment to see how temperatures change under the greenhouse effect.

Materials

- 2 thermometers
- 2 strings

Steps

1. On a hot, sunny day, hang a thermometer in a car. Make sure the windows of the car are closed.

2. Hang another thermometer outside the car.

3. Record the temperatures shown on the thermometers. Then check the temperatures on the thermometers again after two hours.

	At the Beginning	After 2 Hours
Inside the car:	_____°C	_____°C
Outside the car:	_____°C	_____°C

Question

- Why aren't the temperatures shown on the two thermometers the same?

Project Ideas:
Different Kinds of Pollution

Do this project with 2 or 3 classmates. Collect pictures of different kinds of pollution from old magazines, newspapers, or the Internet. Then bring them to school and sort them by the kinds of pollution such as water pollution, air pollution, and land pollution.

You may use a bristol board or large piece of construction paper to paste each set of pictures. Give each board a title. Present the boards to the rest of the class. Then share your views on the topic with your classmates. Let them know how pollution intensifies the effects of global warming.

Project Ideas:

Water Pollution Caused by Oil Spills

Oil tankers sometimes run aground. When the oil spills into the water, it can kill lots of animals. Oil sticks to the feathers of sea birds and the fur of sea lions and seals, making it difficult for the sea birds to fly and the sea lions and seals to keep warm. So, they eventually die. Oil also suffocates fish, shrimps, oysters, and many sea creatures by blocking their intake of oxygen.

Do this experiment. Then you can see what happens to oil when it is mixed with water.

Materials

- a clear plastic bottle
- water
- $\frac{1}{2}$ cup of vegetable oil
- food colouring

Steps

1. Fill about half the bottle with water.
2. Add a few drops of food colouring.
3. Add the vegetable oil.
4. Put the cap back onto the bottle and shake.

Questions

- What happens to the oil?
- Why does this happen?
- How will animals be smothered by oil?

You can see that the oil floats on the coloured water. It is because oil is lighter than water. So, when oil leaks, it spreads to form a thick slick. This suffocates sea creatures.

Project Ideas:

Saving Endangered or Threatened Animals

Some Canadian species are listed by the Scientific Committee on the Station of Endangered Wildlife in Canada as being endangered or threatened.

Look at some examples on the lists. Check the one that you are interested in.

Endangered Species	**Threatened Species**
(wildlife species facing imminent extinction)	(wildlife species likely to become endangered if limiting factors are not reversed)
◯ Vancouver Island Marmot	◯ Woodland Caribou
◯ Bowhead Whale	◯ Beluga Whale
◯ Peary Caribou	◯ Ferruginous Hawk
◯ Spotted Owl	◯ Burrowing Owl
◯ Whopping Crane	◯ White-headed Woodpecker
◯ Leatherback Turtle	◯ Eastern Massasauga Rattlesnake
◯ Aurora Trout	◯ Lake Simcoe Whitefish
◯ Slender Bush Clover	◯ Ginseng
◯ Cucumber Tree	◯ Red Mulberry

Go to libraries to find books about one of the species above that you are interested in. Make a poster by drawing pictures of it on a cardboard. Write sentences to remind people it is time to take action to save this endangered or threatened species before they go extinct.

Project Ideas:
Recycled Items

Make a book to show items that are made from recycled materials.

Steps to Make a Book

1. Get about five pieces of paper and fold them in half.

2. Punch three holes along the folded lines.

3. Tie the paper together with strings.

4. Draw a picture of the recycled item on the left page.

5. Draw lines on the right page for writing about the importance and advantages of using recycled items

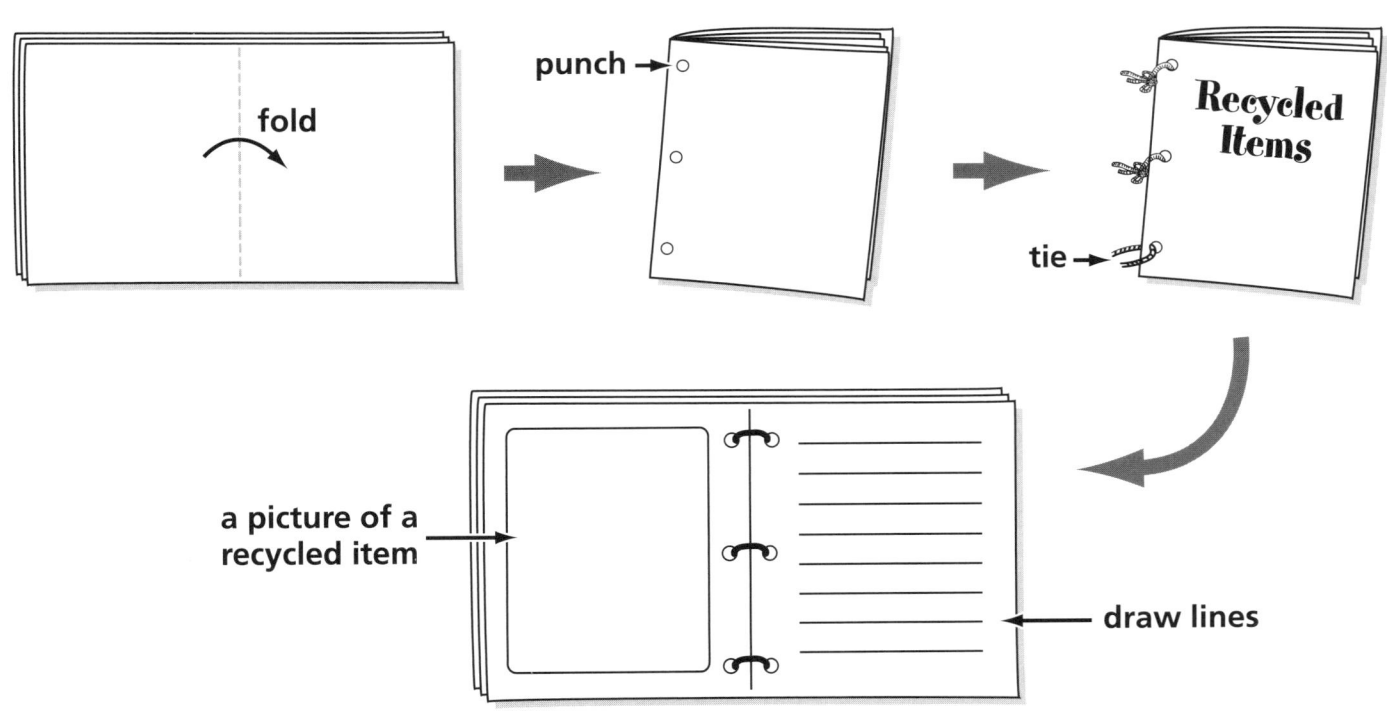

Project Ideas:
Time to Recycle

Through the project, you may have a better idea of what items you can recycle.

 **Make a note.**

List items that can be put in blue boxes and green bins.

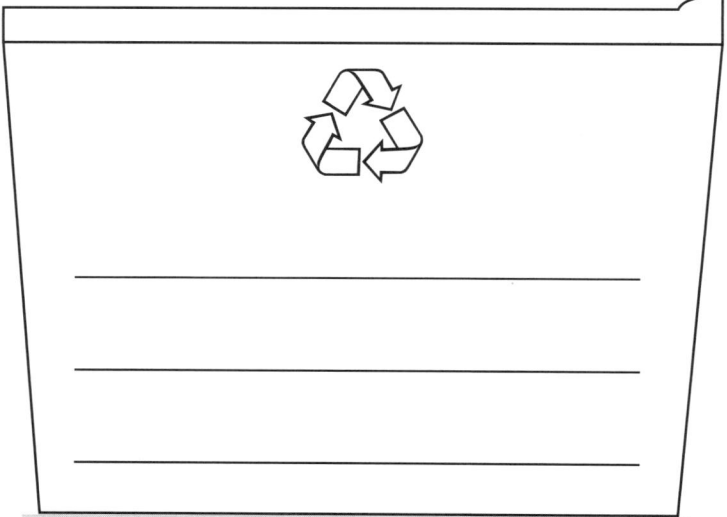

 **Show everyone.**

- Get a cardboard. Draw a big blue box on one side of the cardboard and a big green bin on the other side.

- Find pictures of the items that can be put into blue boxes or green boxes from old magazines, newspapers, and flyers. Then cut and glue them on the correct sides of the cardboard.

- Write a title for each set of pictures if you like.

         Global Warming | G.1-3

p.7

1a. sun's rays   b. atmosphere
  c. reflected   d. trapped

2.
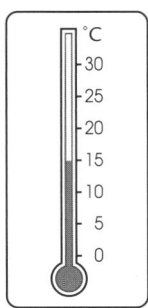

p.8

1. ✗   2. ✗
3. ✔   4. ✔
5. ✔   6. ✔

7. It is because the atmosphere absorbs the ultraviolet rays and keeps the heat from escaping back into space.

8. It would die because the Earth would be too cold and be hit with ultraviolet rays.

p.9

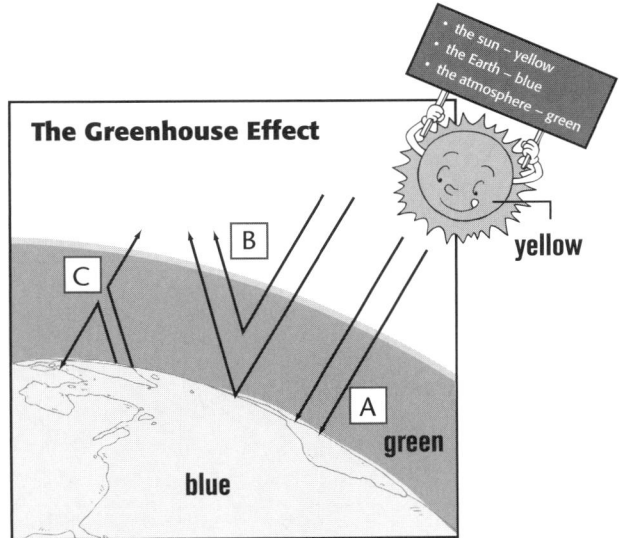

p.11

p.12

1a. solid   b. liquid
2a. gas   b. liquid
 3. solid   4. gas
 5. liquid   6. liquid

p.13

1. Condensation – Water collects as clouds.
   Evaporation – Water changes to gas.
   Precipitation – Water falls as rain.

2.
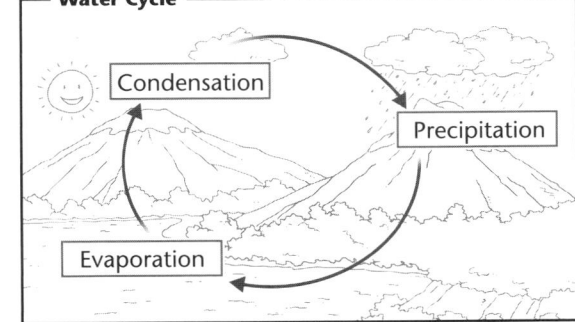

p.15

1. weather
2. climate
3. climate
4. weather
5. climate
6. weather
7. climate

p.16

(Individual answers)

p.17

(Individual answers)

p.19

1. food chains
2. sun
3. Plants
4. Herbivores
5. carnivores
6. sun ; producers ; consumers
7. omnivores

p.20

p.21

1.

2. B
3. A

p. 25

1. ✔
2. ✗
3. ✗
4. ✔
5. ✔
6. The main sources are the burning of fossil fuels and the cutting down of forests.
7. There will be changes in climate. For example, violent storms, heat waves, droughts, and floods may occur more often.

p.26

p.27

(Glue the CO_2 in the atmosphere.)

p.29

1. ✔
2.
3. ✔
4.
5. ✔
6. ✔

p.30

1. Pollution
2. air ; water ; land
3. environment
4. waste
5. Fuels
6. It is the whole world that we live in, including the air we breathe, the water we drink, and the land we live on.
7. Pollution is anything we put back into the environment that harms it or makes it dirty.

p.31

Things We Take from Earth:
wood for houses ; water for drinking ; coal for energy
Things We Put Back into Earth:
poisonous fumes from factories ; garbage from people ; chemicals from farms

p.33

1. land pollution
2. air pollution
3. water pollution
4. air pollution
5. water pollution

p.34

1. water pollution
2. air pollution
3. land pollution
4. water pollution
5. air pollution
6. land pollution

p.35

(Individual answers)

p.39

1. Floods
2. Hurricanes
3. Droughts
4. Wildfires
5. Wildfires may be caused by higher temperatures and greater evaporation.
6. Hurricanes form over warm oceans. The energy comes from the warmer temperature.

p.40

(Individual answers)

p.41

1. Droughts
2. Floods
3. Floods
4. Hurricanes
5. Wildfires
6. Wildfires

p.43

1. A
2. B
3. C
4. A ; B
5. B ; C

p.44

p.45

1. Miami
2. Netherlands
3. Belgium
4. Luxembourg
5. Venice
6. Alexandria

p.47

1. A
2. B
3. C

p.48

1. melt
2. seals
3. food
4. fat
5. reproduce

Answers

p.49

1. Global warming causes the ice to melt.
2. They breed on huge sheets of ice, far from the edges.
3. The chicks may fall into the ocean and drown or freeze to death.

p.51

1. ✗
2. ✔
3. ✗
4. ✔
5. ✔
6. Droughts make crops fail and livestock die.
7. It is a period of abnormally and uncomfortably hot and humid weather.
8. Heat strokes and heat rashes are the illnesses that are related to heat.

p.52

(Colour pictures 1, 2, and 6.)

p.53

1. 3 ; 2 ; 8 ; 9 ; 10
2. Toronto Public Health issues heat alerts.
(Suggested answer)
3. Heat alerts have become more frequent. The number of heat alerts would be greater than 10 in 2015.

p.57

D ; B ; C ; A ;
C ; B

p.58

(Individual answer)

p.59

1. crushed   2. heated   3. bottles

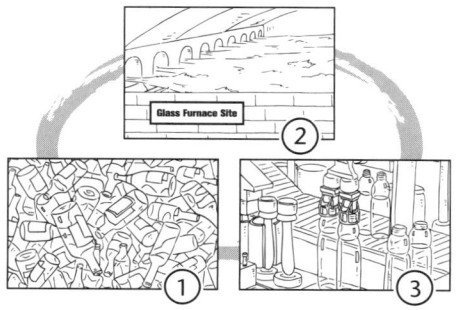

p.61

1. ✔
2.
3. ✔
4. ✔
5.
6. ✔
7. ✔
8.
9. (Individual answer)
10. (Individual answer)

p.62

Plastic: D, G
Metal & Glass: B, F, H
Paper: A, C, E, I, J

p.63

(Colour the slide blue and soft pads green.)